In Case You Weren't Listening...

An Anthology of Memories

By Vivian Newkirk & Friends

THIS WORK IS DEDICATED to

Vivian Newkirk

Sharing her love of family history and knowledge of writing skills, Vivian Newkirk inspired us to mine our own memories. With her patient guidance, we recalled people, places, and events from our youth and composed our stories. What a delight it was to find gold in forgotten fragments of our lives! We are indeed richer for having walked with Vivian through our "memory" class.

INTRODUCTION

IN THE FALL OF 2012, I BEGAN MY FIRST VOLUNTEER
TEACHING ASSIGNMENT "MINING YOUR MEMORIES —
WRITING FAMILY STORIES" at the Ridgeland Public Library.
How pleased I was to spark a desire in a few participants to
write seriously. By the end of eight months of work, four writers
wanted more and began their own group. What a treasure they
have accumulated! The selections chosen for this book are
amusing, poignant, serious. Some have brought tears to our eyes.

My deep-felt appreciation to Andy, Jeanne, Sharlie and Gloria
for your patience and your willingness to open your hearts on
the page and create memorable stories your family and friends
will enjoy for years to come.

When Andy Oldham presented us a copy of his new novel, he
suggested as a group we publish our stories we shared monthly.
Taking the responsibility of preparing the manuscript for
printing, Andy encouraged us to stay the course. We owe our
deepest gratitude for his direction.

Hearty thanks to Nan Crosby, head librarian at Ridgeland
Public Library, who suggested the class and helped with
publicity and a meeting room; and to Tammy Terry of the
Madison Public Library, who took up the reins for the private
group and provided meeting space. Without your enthusiasm for
what we wanted to accomplish, we would not have advanced to
printing our book.

~ Vivian Newkirk

Contents

Dedication

Introduction

Jeanne Smith Kelly   11

    I Didn't Listen   12

    Feast Week   14

    Remembering Mama   18

    Good-bye Santa   20

    Mamoo's Marriage   23

    Glimpses of Heaven   25

    Brother Jim   27

    Lost In The Memories   32

Gloria C. Lightwine   33

    The Fab Four – 1964   34

    Clothes Do Not Make the Person   35

    Fresh From the Garden   38

    Scary Hooded Creatures   40

Sharlie McGriff   43

    My Tree   44

    Book Buddies   46

    Those Eyes   52

Andy Oldham   53

    One Delicious Memory   54

    Hunting Fiasco   57

    Labor Day   59

The Night Bessie Bumped Her Head   63

The Dumbest Thing I Have Ever Done   66

Whoops   68

Vivian Newkirk   71

Tuberculosis Scare   72

The Argument   75

Miss Velsor, Peggy and Me   77

Lessons In Organic Gardening   89

My First Watch   82

Jeanne Smith Kelly

Retired after 38 years as a classroom teacher, Jeanne enjoys reading mysteries, teaching her adult Sunday School class, writing and spending time with family. Her poetry has appeared in numerous publications, including Mississippi Poetry Society's journals, *Voices International, Decision and Encore,* the anthology of the National Federation of State Poetry Societies.

<u>Favorite Quote:</u>
The greatest glory in living lies not in never falling, but in rising every time we fall.
~ Ralph Waldo Emerson

I DIDN'T LISTEN

ROCKING IN A WOODEN CHAIR on the front
porch
Chewing on a plug of Red Man tobacco,
My grandfather talked, droning like cicadas
On a summer night.
His favorite topic: politics.
       He expounded on why he never voted
       for even one Republican in his entire life.
He talked about work:
       Success in life's not guaranteed by
       education;
       We all had to start at the bottom and
       work up,
       Even with fancy college degrees.
He talked about his youth:
       Prospecting for timber for the family
       Camping with Indians on the Pascagoula
       River.
       Plowing fields behind oxen and mules,
       Cooking sugar cane to make molasses.
He talked about our ancestors—
       Irish peddlers who found their way
       To South Carolina, Georgia, western
       Alabama,
       Finally settling near State Line,
       Mississippi.
       They were Browns, Smiths, Walleys,
       Hintons.

He talked and talked and talked.

> As his dim blue eyes gathered memories,
> He cataloged branches of our family tree,
> His voice still strong for a man of ninety-
> three.

As he talked,
I nodded, sometimes smiled,

> Not really listening to what he said—
> He said so much.

When his voice was forever silenced at ninety-four,
I wandered among the graves at Frisco Cemetery
Where the headstones displayed names of
> ancestors:
Smith, Brown, Walley, Hinton.
I wished I had listened as he shared those stories
About his life and family history.
The only one who knew all that was he.

FEAST WEEK

THE ONLY TIME I REMEMBER CELEBRATING THANKSGIVING WITH DADDY'S parents was when Granddaddy had a heart attack the week before Thanksgiving. At the time I was only eight and did not realize that our reason for going then was related to my grandfather's health. He was at home feeling fine by the time we finally arrived, worn out from our 600-mile drive from Jonesboro, Tennessee, to Perry County, Mississippi.

I wasn't used to seeing the farm in the fall. All my experiences there had been in the summer when vegetables and corn were harvested. The fallow fields flanking the lane to the house seemed cold and unwelcoming. Even the tung-oil trees had shed their leaves. However, as we drove past the barn, we caught sight of my cousin Billy herding cattle in for their evening feeding. Pigs grunted, anticipating their trough of slop, and chickens clucked their way to the hen house.

Daddy stopped the car to ask Billy how Granddaddy was doing. "Oh, he's fine," he said. "In fact, he came home from the hospital this morning. Doc Fridge said it was just a mild heart attack and he should be good as new before long. Grandma's been lookin' for ya'll to get here all day."

The chilly November evening discouraged folks from sitting on the porch, but once we got into Grandma's kitchen, it felt like home. She was frying pork chops in the big iron skillet. Aunt Mary was pouring black-eyed peas and turnip greens into serving bowls.

When the cornbread and pork chops were done, I went to the front room to call the men and boys to the table. Granddaddy took his usual chair next to the head of the table and, when the rest of the group found a place, he said his usual prayer. No matter who was visiting—preachers included—he sat in the same place and prayed the same prayer: "Heavenly Father, we thank you for these and for all other blessings. In the name of your son Jesus, Amen."

A Special Day at the Country School

Because we arrived on Monday, we had days to fill before the Thanksgiving gathering. On Wednesday, my cousin Virginia invited me to go to school with her. An eighth grader, she assured me that I would know many of the students there because I was kin to them. The Brewer school had only two classrooms, one for grades one through four and the other, grades five through eight. After eighth grade the students went to Richton High School. I felt as if I were visiting Tom Sawyer's school as Mr. Carey, the teacher, began by listing assignments on the board, then checked homework. The antique desks had lift-up lids.

Just as Virginia had promised, I saw familiar faces, and I looked forward to recess and lunch. I stayed with Virginia, and Mr. Carey let me pull my desk close to her so I, a third grader, could keep up with what was going on. Although he humored me, I knew I wasn't up to eighth-grade level. At recess, I played with the younger cousins and learned more about life at a country school. The bathrooms were outdoor toilets, four for the girls and three for the boys. Since it was a warm day for November, we ate lunch outside. There was a snack shed where people could buy drinks and snacks, but almost everyone brought their own lunch complete with a thermos filled with milk, tea, or Kool-Aid. We played Red Rover, jacks, and Simon Says. The boys played baseball or just threw basketballs at a goal set up on the playground, the only play equipment there.

Rooster Attack

After school the bus, driven by my sixteen-year-old cousin Shorty, dropped me off back at Grandma's. I walked out to the barn, where nothing much was happening in mid-afternoon. Then I took a turn toward the chicken house. The hens were loose in the yard clucking around, just waiting for Grandma to feed them.

Grandma called to me out the back door, "Jeannie Lin, see if you can find some eggs from the nests in the hen house. I need them for cornbread." I grabbed an egg basket and found some unguarded eggs. As I started back to the house, a big red rooster flew at me, squawking. I screamed as loud as I could and tried to run away. Neck feathers ruffled, wings and toes spread, he flew at me again, and I screamed louder calling for help. Grandma ran out flapping her apron at her unruly bird, yelling, "Shoo, Shoo!"

Luckily, the eggs survived because I kept the basket upright. At first, Grandma laughed at me because I was shaking from fright after the riled rooster episode. "You didn't try to pet that fellow, did you?" When I began to cry, she was more sympathetic. "Shug, the rooster is just protecting his hens. What would you like for me to do to him?"

"Kill him, and cook him for Thanksgiving," I sobbed.

"Well, we need the rooster to take care of the hens, but I'll pen him up if he gives you any more trouble." I settled down and came into the kitchen where preparations for the Thanksgiving feast had already begun. Mama was busy cutting up onions and celery for dressing to go with the fat hens Grandma would bake the next morning. Aunt Mary was beating cake batter. Inside the

16

kitchen safe, I found a cold biscuit to munch on and went to the front porch to swing.

Granddaddy pulled us out of bed at sunrise the next morning. We needed to get breakfast early and get the chores done because the entire family-aunts, uncles, and cousins-- would arrive before dinner.

A Real Feast

Arrive they did, loaded with assorted meats, cakes, pies, congealed salads, and vegetables along with card tables and folding chairs. Food covered the top of the deep freeze, the kitchen counters, a back porch table and the long kitchen table. Aunt Mary made several gallons of tea. With the food came kids to play with. The boys ran the length of the lane and back yelling and jeering at each other. The girls stayed closer to the house helping out with the babies.

Finally, the dinner bell rang. But wait! Until the grown-ups were served and seated, children could not fix their plates. Finally we got our food and headed to the front porch. The teenagers claimed the screened porch on the back of the house. Besides having plenty of other children to play with, I enjoyed the food—especially desserts. Yes, desserts plural! Mama was preoccupied caring for my brothers and visiting with the women. She did not notice how many I sampled. With choices like chocolate cake, coconut cake, spice cake, peach pie, chess pie, pecan pie, pumpkin pie, potato pie, chocolate pie, I had found dessert heaven.

By mid-afternoon, families began heading back to their homes, full and happy. At supper we dined on leftovers. On the long trip home, I dreamed about the most memorable Thanksgiving ever. I hadn't even noticed that no one brought turkey.

REMEMBERING MAMA

AS I WROTE MY MOTHER'S OBITUARY,
reducing her lengthy life to a few paragraphs
of black ink on newsprint,
her essence escaped standard format
of conventional etiquette's rules.
More comfortable in pink fleece sweat suits
than the royal blue dress she's buried in,
she thought trying to look regal was "putting on airs."
Chalk dust in her veins,
she taught well past retirement age.
She hated cooking,
served most meals on plastic plates,
believed nutrition mattered more
than gourmet flavor or "presentation."
She held her money tightly—hid little stashes of green bills
beneath undies and nighties in her dresser drawers.
After moving to a nursing home,
she kept pennies in a plastic jar deep in her closet,
the bank for old men's nightly poker games;

but she never played poker.
She loved
chocolate melting on her tongue,
wind blowing her hair back as she faced the sun,
the color yellow,
the scent of gardenias,
cats purring on her lap,
show music and church music.
In her dying days, mellow tones
of George Beverly Shea's
"His Eye is on the Sparrow"
soothed her painful passing.
Those who loved her will miss
her flashing brown eyes,
her laughter, and the crusty mask
covering her sweet, gentle soul.

GOOD-BYE, SANTA

SANTA WAS REAL. We had proof in a picture taken in Parks-Belk Department Store in Johnson City, Tennessee. It captured me at five and my younger brother Pat at two sitting in Santa's lap. Pat looked like a typical toddler, completely oblivious to the significance of the "jolly old elf." I, on the other hand, knew all about Santa's magic. He'd bring me whatever I asked, and my list was etched in my mind: a bride doll that could walk, a giant box of crayons, and a pedal car. Furthermore, I wanted the list to be a special secret between Santa and me.

Daddy had to apply pressure to get me to share that list. He said that Santa always asked parents' approval before he would deliver the toys. I finally told him what I'd asked for. As for my little brother, he only wanted one thing—a "dangle-ance," his term for a fire truck featuring a bell that its little drivers could jingle. Santa faithfully brought us everything we wanted.

A year later I once again prepared a list, and my parents took us to see Santa. My big wish was for a doll that came with a set of rollers for its lifelike hair. On Christmas Eve, our family walked the three blocks to Jonesboro's courthouse square. There firemen dressed as elves gave children bags filled with fruit and candy. When we got home, Daddy read "A Visit from Santa" three or four times. His voice rose and fell dramatically. He whispered, "Twas the night before Christmas, when all through the house, not a creature was stirring, not even a mouse." When he said, "Out on the lawn, there arose such a clatter," his deep voice began to swell as Santa urged his reindeer: "On Dasher, On, Dancer, . . ." Finally he boomed, "Down the chimney St. Nicholas came with a bound." Then he quietly told about Santa's filling all of the stockings. As he concluded, "Happy Christmas to all and to all a good night," Daddy added a resounding, "Ho! Ho! Ho!"

Filled with excitement, I had a terrible time trying to go to sleep. Wide-eyed I watched moonlight shadows reflected through tree branches onto my bedroom wall. Sure the silhouettes were Santa and his reindeer, I stayed as still as a statue so he would not know I was awake. The next morning I raced downstairs to confirm that my Christmas dreams had once again been granted.

Excitedly I told Mama and Daddy about seeing the reindeer and the sleigh during the night. They argued that Santa would never let himself or his reindeer and sleigh be seen by a wakeful child. "But I really did see it on the balcony!" I insisted. To keep my brother from hearing the conversation to come, my parents took me to their bedroom for a talk.

There Daddy informed me that I could not have seen the reindeer and sleigh because Santa was not real. What I had seen was just a reflection of tree branches in the moonlight. At first, I did not believe them. Santa had to be real because I had sat in his lap and told him what I wanted, and he had brought me everything I asked for. "Where did the toys come from if Santa isn't real?" I wanted to know.

Daddy's answer to that shocked me. He said, "I buy your toys for you. Santa is just pretend for little children. You are old enough to know the difference between real and pretend."

Although I accused him of not telling the truth, I finally accepted the fact that there was no Santa. I knew he and Mama were serious when Mama cautioned me, "Don't tell your brothers the secret. Little children enjoy the magic of getting their wishes granted." I regretted having told them about seeing the reindeer, and I never really enjoyed styling my new doll's hair. The myth was "busted."

When that fairy tale died, the best part of childhood ended for me. I didn't feel gratitude to my parents when I learned that they had provided the miraculous toys; I was angry because they had taken away a magical illusion.

MAMOO'S MARRIAGE

FRONT PORCH GOSSIPING BORED HER;
    She often stayed alone,
    But home was just too lonely
    Once her children were grown.
    She read of others' adventures
    Until her eyes grew tired from the strain.
    Then she'd flag down a silver Greyhound
    And travel to try to keep sane.
    "Do you live on the bus?" asked a grandchild.
    "No, Sugar, but traveling can be
    lots of fun," Mamoo answered and smiled.
    Her odysseys led her to one remote place
    Where she taught three grades in one room,
    But even the chatter of children
    Could not erase her lonely gloom.
    But there she met a backwoods man
    Who brought excitement and joy to her life.
    With flowers and candy he courted her
    Until she agreed to be his wife.
    Her family couldn't understand
    What she saw in that grizzly old man,
    But for the rest of her life she lived with him,
    Even accepting his rude mannered clan.
    Who knows why two people fall in love
    Or where they find companionship?
    What force persuades a wandering widow
    To call an end to her Greyhound trip?
    A common old geezer who'd spit on the floors

In his dog-trot house with no screen doors
Won the heart of a lady, cultured, refined—
One longing for romance enough to be blind.

GLIMPSES OF HEAVEN WITH MAMA

WHEN I SEE DAFFODILS IN BLOOM,
I think of Mama praying while
I planted bulbs. As if in church,
With reverence she thanked the Lord
For beauty they would bring in spring,
Asking that all who saw the golden flowers
Would be blessed by His creation.
Gaudy summer hibiscus blossoms
Also remind me of Mama .
She loved the vivid fuchsias,
Reds, oranges, and yellows
although each bloom lasted only one day,
A day God made to rejoice and be glad in.
When pear trees put on their autumn show,
I remember Mama's joy. Though stooped
With age, she picked up fallen leaves,
to craft a red-and-gold collage for my
grandchildren,
to show them the glory of God,
who created such colorful beauty.
In winter I remember Mama,
White-haired, thick sweatered,
Shivering against blasts of cold air.
She still turned her face toward the sun
From her nursing-home wheelchair.
She delighted in visitors bearing poinsettias,
Singing Christmas carols, and decorating the tree--
Thrilling her heart one last time.

All year long I remember Mama,
And now I see her as she truly was.
Though dementia clouded her memories,
She praised the creator with her whole soul
gaining glimpses of her eternity:
Forever walking in the garden with God.

BROTHER JIM

FISHER OF TROUT AND OF MEN, My Father, Jim Aaron often said, "Country People, especially farmers, are the finest people on earth."

Tall and handsome, he had wavy black hair and blue eyes. Looking good was important to him. He liked his shirts starched and his dress shoes polished. His booming bass voice rang clear without a microphone in his fifty-plus years as a preacher.

When he was born in 1914, my grandmother named him Jim Aaron Smith. When he joined the National Guard, he learned that the doctor who delivered him wrote *James* on his birth certificate. After he left Richton, Mississippi, and became a preacher, he used "James A." for his official name. Grandma did not appreciate his name- changing one bit. She said, "I have another son named James. People would think I was crazy if I gave the same name to two sons!" At least the other one, James Melton, was always called by his middle name, thus saving her from being thought ignorant. She staunchly supported my father's calling to the ministry. "I also named you Aaron, the head of the priestly tribe in the Bible," she told him.

Grandma had a lot of pride in herself and her family, and she passed that trait along to her boys. My daddy got a double dose of pride, making him quite egotistical at times. He had been a sickly child, and the whole family coddled him because of it. His ten-year-old sister died of appendicitis when he was two years old. Because of his puniness, the loss of his sister, and his position as the baby of the family, he "ruled the roost." However, when he was ten, his reign as baby of the family ended when his spirited younger sister Mary was born. He once said, "My family spent the first few years of my life spoiling me, and for the rest of my childhood they tried to beat the rottenness out of me, but the beating didn't work. I can't help it if I'm spoiled."

The family farm required that everyone work to keep it going. The pond gave them both food and fun. Throughout his life, my father enjoyed fishing. When church members invited him to use ponds or lakes on their property, he usually accepted. He seemed to have the most fun when we lived in Jonesborough, Tennessee. He never missed an opportunity to go to the mountains with friends to fish for rainbow trout. On one of those trips, he led a friend to accept Christ, an experience that thrilled him.

Opinionated and argumentative, he learned how to debate at his family dinner table. Granddaddy, James C. "Bud" Smith, wanted to make his children think and often started political discussions. If they offered an opinion, he asked questions, making them defend their point of view. Consequently, Daddy thought conversation meant arguing. He never understood why people got angry when he disagreed with them. In his own mind he was right about everything.

I learned not to challenge him unless I could prove my point. When I was in fourth grade learning about our U.S. Presidents, Daddy insisted that all of our greatest leaders had been Baptist. I disagreed, saying that Lincoln was a Presbyterian. As proof I showed him the *World Book Encyclopedia*'s list of Presidents and their religion. Facing the evidence, he said, "Well, back then Presbyterians were just like Baptists anyway."

When he was fifteen, he drove across a railroad track and a train hit the car. Thankfully, his passengers, his sister-in-law Myrtle and niece Catherine, had no serious injuries. After the impact, the train kept moving for a bit and dragged young Jim down the track. He survived with a broken arm and a lot of cuts and bruises. Almost torn from his head, his ear had to be reattached. After the wreck his friends nicknamed him "Freight Train."

He was always a fearless driver. In spite of his recklessness, he had surprisingly few smash-ups. If he had an accident, he always insisted that the other driver caused it. It took a lot of prayer to ride with him. He drove too fast and darted in and out of highway lanes. He thought his skills equal to those of a race-car driver. In the Smokey Mountains and later in the Rockies, he hugged the outer edge on curves, laughing because Mother and I were afraid we'd roll down the cliffs.

When Daddy was eighty, he took his new pastor to lunch. He reasoned that the person who might preach his funeral needed to know who he was. After they returned safely to the church office, the preacher said, "I need to make Brother Jim our minister of evangelism. A ride with him will make you anxious to get right with God."

Although my father insisted on the superiority of his rural upbringing, some of his decisions suggested otherwise. For example, he listened to recordings of Franklin D. Roosevelt's voice and copied the President's speech patterns to help correct his rural Mississippi twang.

In another instance, he imposed his educated standards on his first music director. After he received his B.A. degree from Mississippi College and his Master of Theology at Southern Seminary in Louisville, Kentucky, Daddy considered himself cultured. In his first full-time pastorate in Corinth, Mississippi, he threw out the Stamps-Baxter songbooks preferred by his part-time music director in favor of the standard *Broadman* Hymnal published by the Southern Baptist Convention. He dismissed the gospel songs, saying, "That's not real music. It's not worshipful." To this day, Brewer Baptist Church, his home church, has two hymnals—the standard *Baptist Hymnal* and another one containing southern gospel tunes with a beat that can raise the rafters.

In a further indication that he wanted to correct any deficiencies of his rural background, he married my mother. Her father, Dr. M.O. Patterson, was head of the Bible department at Mississippi College and a highly respected theologian during the 1920's and 1930's. Ironically, Dr. Patterson's background was similar to Daddy's. He grew up in a rural community near Columbia and later married my grandmother, who had been educated at the Boston Conservatory of Music. Her family provided money for him to earn his theology doctorate after he and my grandmother married. When Daddy met his role model's daughter Mary Lin, her flashing brown eyes won his heart. It helped that she had her father's passion and devotion to God.

Maintaining a close relationship with his family was important to my dad. Although we had little time to get to know his people because we didn't live near Mississippi in our childhood, he insisted that we love them just because they were kin. When I asked how we could love people we didn't know, he didn't have a good answer. We loved kinfolks just because we were blood relatives.

When Daddy was ninety, he bought his tombstone and staked out his final resting place in Frisco Cemetery. He wanted to be sure that he got a spot near his parents. He didn't want a niece or nephew or anyone else to get his rightful place. He had the marker placed beside that of his brother, James Melton. Seeing his own headstone there in order, Daddy gave a satisfied nod. Etched on the stone was his birth-certificate name with a title added: *Rev.* James Aaron Smith. The title *Reverend* distinguished him from the other James Smiths buried nearby.

LOST IN THE MEMORIES

AN OLD BLACK-AND WHITE PHOTOGRAPH
shows how tall and handsome
my father was in his prime,
his vanity caught in lifted head.
Mama looked young and pretty,
hair still dark, skin unwrinkled,
smiling brightly for the camera, baby in her lap;
my brother and I stand beside her;
he leans toward her for security.
This little piece of our history
captures us at a golden wedding celebration
for my grandparents,
their cow pasture in the background.
Both they and the farm are long gone.
Even my parents have passed on.
Although they always seemed ancient to me,
a photographer froze them
as young adults
while the careless child I was shyly smiled,
forever waiting to grow up.

Gloria C. Lightwine

Gloria Jean Clark Lightwine was born and reared in the foothills of Virginia's Blue Ridge Mountains. After college, her dreams of adventure were realized by serving as a volunteer in Colombia with Peace Corps. She worked in health education on the Mexican-US border for a few years and obtained a MPH from UNC-Chapel Hill. After marriage, she lived in Nicaragua and worked in rural health clinics. A resident of Mississippi since 1975, she retired from the University of Mississippi Medical Center. Now she spends her time writing and collecting stories of her memories.

Favorite Quote:

Attention is love, what we must give children, mothers, fathers, pets, our friends, the news, the woes of others. What we want to change we curse and then pick up a tool. Bless whatever you can with your eyes and hands and tongue. If you can't bless it get ready to make it new. ~Marge Piercy

THE FAB FOUR - 1964

"I WANNA HOLD YOUR HAND -and-and, I Wanna Hold Your Hand." The strange music filled the hot, muggy air of the room at a party in Barranquilla, Colombia. It was during the later part of 1964. Some Peace Corps Volunteers from outlying areas were in for rest and recreation. I, along with my Peace Corps partner, Brucie Richardson, was in town to pick up mail, get our monthly check, buy some provisions and eat. We lived three hours via bus down the Magdalena River from Barranquilla. We usually came to town about once a month. Two new volunteers, Bob Cutri and Gordie Munson, had recently been assigned to Campo de la Cruz about an hour up river from our village of Suan.

They were in town, as well, and at the party. Gordie brought a LP record with this new kind of music. He was gyrating with arms flinging, legs jumping up and down and hips swaying! All of us were just watching in amazement. The music and lyrics were sort of catchy. The record played on: "Can't Buy Me Love", "Twist and Shout", "She Loves You", "Please Please Me." Soon all of us joined in with movement to the rhythms, moving anyway we wanted. Gordie told us that this band named "The Beatles" was all the rage back home. Of course, the rest is history.

As I am writing this in early 2015, it is 50 years ago that The Beatles were discovered and made history with their music, lyrics, and movies.

CLOTHES DO NOT MAKE THE PERSON

CLAD IN RAGGEDY JEANS, an old tattered army jacket and a Halloween wig made of yellow threads with lime-green streaks, I was ready to ride. My husband, older daughter and I headed to the airport to pick up the younger daughter. They were not too happy with my appearance and voiced their opinion on the entire expedition. The first semester of college had been a long three-and-a-half months, and all of us were anxious to see her.

I can see the question marks flying around your head wondering why in the world I would pull such a silly stunt when I was on my way to meet the daughter I loved so. However, her history includes a pattern of exercising poor judgment in a variety of circumstances. I cannot, even to this day forget the misfortune of one such grievous and regrettable decision. Like any parent with a child in high school, what I believed to be poor choices in appropriate attire, along with hairstyle and hair colors caused conflict.

Just before leaving for her freshman year of college, she took it upon herself to dye her hair indigo black. When I arrived home from work and walked into her room, I was appalled at the sight of jet black hair framing her pale face. She looked like a zombie. What had *she done*? I stared at first but knew I could not say a word. Our eyes locked, she let out an uncertain grin, and I ran to the garage shaken by her wild and careless decision. Uncontrollable tears ran down my cheeks while I contemplated how she had undermined all thoughts of what *I* wanted for her. She surprised me with her presence as she walked into the garage. Blubbering, I turned away and wiped the droplets from

35

my eyes. It was to no avail. She had already seen the wet tissues *and* the despair. Memories gyrated through my head like a tornado of confusion while I recalled her frequent comments on how unethical and unwarranted it is to judge others by their appearance. Outside appearance is not important, she would say; seeing the inside of a person is utmost. Frankly, she reminded me that I had once believed in that same precept when I was her age. The heart and mind should be appraised; appearance does not determine character, but then, how many people really do that?

Wrapping her arms around me the two of us wept consoling tears of grief. I had not understood what was going through her mind when I had a closer look at her now- ebony hair. She had beautiful hair, and now it was ruined. I had not taken the time to ask how she felt about her decision; instead, I ran. Only when she came to me did I appreciate how *she* felt and that she knew she had made the wrong decision. She did not like her choice. It hadn't turned out as she expected; she needed consoling more than anyone. It was her heart that allowed me to understand that she was young and inquisitive. She had made a bad decision, and now we both would live with it, at least for a short time. She continued to make strange choices for hair at college.

Experiences like that explain why I decided to dress in this silly, unconventional manner when meeting my daughter in a public place. Maybe, *just maybe*, it would shake her up a little when she saw her Mom in a ridiculous wig. Perhaps the sight might jar her into thinking more about her own choices.

While we walked through the terminal I turned to look for my husband and daughter. It seems they were keeping their distance from me as I spotted them walking on the other side. I smiled and continued toward the waiting area. Upon arrival I found a seat between two well-dressed women. One glanced at me and then connected with the other. As if a director had raised his wand for the choir to stand, each stood and left in unison. I could feel the proverbial *look*. The ever present arbitrators of justice each seemed to be looking straight through me, wondering why I was dressed like a clown. I could hear the whispers of inquiry one to another among others in the waiting area. I acted as normal as possible. My husband and daughter were nowhere to be found. They were *not* going to own up to knowing me dressed like this. I nonchalantly sat there waiting.

Upon the plane's arrival, husband and daughter appeared from nowhere, and the three of us walked to the disembarking area. I was nervous when she walked through the arrival gate with a refreshing smile on her face. She looked wonderful. She was dressed the way I had always wanted her to be. She had grown up in these short months. I was so proud. Her eyes locked on mine, but she went to her father first, wrapped her arms around him and gave him a large hug. I waited in anticipation in my yellow-with-lime-green-striped wig while she gave the same greeting to her sister.

She turned to me, smiled, wrapped her arms around my neck, and embraced me with the warmest hug she had ever given me, and a verbal communiqué to "take off the wig." Of course, it was my intention to keep it on. Walking down the concourse toward the exit to the parking lot, she tried several times to remove it, but I managed to keep it on my head. I reminded her with each effort that it was not the clothes that make a person, but the heart. I was amazed after these months of absence that even though I wore silly wig, she still laughed and took it all in stride.

37

FRESH FROM THE GARDEN

GREEN PEAS AND TOMMY TOES -that's what I remember about the garden plot next to our house on the Smith River in Martinsville, VA. A large Black Walnut tree grew in that plot on the bank of the river that flowed past our property. I never liked Black Walnuts even in the special cakes made for the fall holidays.

My sister and I were very young-maybe three and four years old. We had a cow named Ole Bess. She rummaged through the grassy lot eating and chewing her cud until it was time for her to give up her life to put meat on our table. I remember crying as she was being slaughtered. It's hard to believe my parents allowed us to be in the presence of slaughtering. This was all part of my growing up.

After Bess left the lot, Daddy plowed it up for use as a garden in the spring and summer. Marie and I wandered through the pea and tomato patches, eating as we played among the rows of vegetables. I remember the wonderful taste of green peas. We pulled the pod from the vine and crushed it with our little fingers. When open, three or four peas were easily plucked from the pod. Yum . . . green, tender, sweet and just a little bit crunchy. I could eat them all day. To this day, I do not like canned peas or green peas that are overcooked.

Tommy Toes were tiny, round tomatoes, classified today as a variety of cherry tomato. They originated from the Arkansas Ozarks in the 1930's and now are considered an heirloom plant.

I remember they grew on long vines that swirled all over the stakes holding them up and all over the adjacent plants. We plucked and ate them along with the peas. So juicy and sweet! I bet Mother had a time getting all those drippy stains out of our flour-sack dresses when she washed them in the galvanized wash tub on the scrub board with water drawn up in a bucket from our well.

Marie in Front of the Garden

Later on, as we grew into elementary school ages, the lot was left vacant and kept mowed. This was our ball field and the center of play for all the children on our road. When I was twelve, we moved to 1429 Rivermont Heights, leaving behind some of the magic of our childhood.

SCARY HOODED CREATURES

MY DAUGHTER ALLISON and I said good-bye to my husband David at the Jackson airport. He was headed for a business trip. Still new to Mississippi, I was always sad when he had to leave town. We had not yet made many friends. Allison was three years old, and I was pregnant with our second child in that summer of 1976.

We lived in Madison County. The airport was in rural Rankin County. David always liked to take the Ross Barnett Reservoir back roads on his way to the airport. I was not familiar with the area; however, I thought I could find my way back to Ridgeland. How hard could it be?

After we kissed and hugged David goodbye, I drove off in the taxicab-yellow 1974 Plymouth sedan trying to find our way back home. Allison was safely in her car seat and chattering away as usual. I entered the boulevard leaving the airport and then had no idea which way to go. I drove until I saw a sign pointing to the Reservoir and followed the arrow. Then I noticed another sign indicating the city of Brandon was near, and I followed that arrow. I thought I could orient myself from the town and at least get to I-20 and find my way to I-55.

I drove on and on. Allison asked me every few minutes, "Where are we?" I did not know. I could see nothing except fields and narrow back roads. Soon Allison crawled up beside me and positioned herself on the fold-down arm between the front seats. We were lost in the wilds of Rankin County.

All of a sudden in the distance, a group of people appeared on the horizon at a crossroad. They wore long white robes with cape-like swags hanging from the back of their shoulders. Their long, wide sleeves draped at the wrist. They had on white hats with pointed tops. As we drew closer, I could see eight or ten of them. I realized then who this group was. The Ku Klux Klan. Here in 1976. What to do! Why were they here!

I was scared to death! Here I was in the middle of nowhere with a three year old and another child in my belly. What were those creatures doing out there? How could I protect us? Fear griped my body and soul.

Allison kept asking who those people were and why were they wearing white robes. My mind kept spinning. There was nothing to do but forge ahead. As we got closer, I could see the "creatures" held out coffee cans asking for donations at the stop sign. Whew! With car windows rolled up, I nodded my head and slowly drove past this dreaded group. I did not know where I was, but I kept driving. The fear I felt that day blotted out my recollection of how we made it home. But find a way, I did.

"You are our living link to the past. Tell your grandchildren the story of the struggles waged, at home and abroad. Of sacrifices made for freedom's sake. And tell them your own story as well — because [everybody] has a story to tell."

President George H.W. Bush

State of the Union Address, 1990

Sharlie McGriff

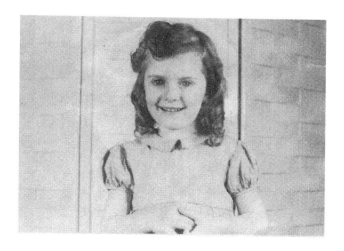

Sharlie McGriff taught high school and college English throughout her adult years. She also was administrative assistant to the director of Recreation and Parks for the City of Ridgeland where she resides. She has a son, a daughter, and four grandchildren. Books are her passion.

<u>Favorite Quote</u>
Ancora imparo (I am still learning.)
Michelangelo, at age eighty-seven.

MY TREE

ON THE RIGHT SIDE of the front yard stood a tree with a thick, gnarled wisteria vine wrapped around its trunk and branches. Though the tree was unremarkable, maybe a beech or an elm, it provided hours and hours of entertainment for my friends and me. The vines allowed my playmates and me at the age of five to climb the tree with ease. We sat and played pretend games among the grape-clustered purple wisteria flowers and thick green leaves of the tree.

Wilma, my neighbor and best friend, was only three when we first dared to climb the tree. We played "Pat and Liz;" I always insisted on being Pat because she was my much-adored, special first cousin. We prepared meals with the "grapes" and served them on the palm-sized green leaves.

Throughout the following years, our imaginations grew with us. Wilma, in her sweet-natured way, let me be the bossy one and we began our pretend scenario that could go on all day. Sometimes Mother brought us peanut butter sandwiches which we ate in our hidden spots high in the limbs. Kathy and I were cowboys under the tree, dressed in our authentic Roy Rogers and Gene Autry cowboy outfits. (I still have that Roy Rogers outfit.) The rooted, grassless yard below the tree allowed us to "dig to China" or to make mud pies.

My fascination with the circus provided clumsy attempts at vine-swinging. The packed dirt and roots below the tree hurt when I fell. Even though several falls knocked the breath out of me, either determined, or stupid, I tried again. A tree limb became a high wire and we tottered out and back, always holding on to a branch above. Our raw carrot or a banana snack tasted just like cotton candy high in the imaginary big top.

The tree was where we ran and hid from Buddy and Jimmy if time permitted us to climb high enough. Sometimes they trapped us there and we stayed prisoners for what seemed like hours. Sooner or later Mother came out to check on us or to call us in to eat, and the boys slunk away.

Cozy in my tree among the leaves, hidden from view of passing cars and people walking by on the sidewalk, I was content. Even now, whenever I see a wisteria vine, I am five years old again, looking at my small world from high in my tree, sheltered and happy.

BOOK BUDDIES

MY FATHER'S ABSENCE was the norm in our household and his

letters were a familiar and comforting form of communication. He worked away from home in the 1940's and 1950's; he was a civil engineer and went where the work called him, returning home on weekends. He wrote to Mother and me as often as time allowed, painting pictures of his surroundings and sometimes referencing a story that he read to me the weekend before.

Daddy wrote postcards and letters to Mother and some just to me when he served with the U.S. Engineers in the Army during World War II. My first memories of him were those brief furloughs at home reading to me as I sat in his lap in the rocking chair. His homesick letters from Fort Belvoir, Virginia, came often. I was too young to read, but I recognized his formal script.

When the postman handed me the mail as I sat on the steps waiting, Daddy's card or letter lay on top of the stack. Dashing into the house, slamming the screen door, I called, "Ma-ma, Daddy wrote a letter." I sat at the kitchen table. She at once stopped whatever she was doing to read. He closed with "give Mama a hug from me" or "take care of Mama."

When at home, Daddy read to me every night: *Tom Sawyer*, *Huck Finn, Bambi, Alice in Wonderland, National Velvet, Black Beauty,* and *Toby Tyler*. The stories stirred my imagination. They were the basis of my daily pretend games as I grew. My love for the circus in particular involved activities which he encouraged by making me wooden stilts. My friends and I practiced every day walking and rolling on an old oil barrel he found for us.

Permanent photographs in my mind are the few times he took me with him when he was working close to home. We wandered among fields and woods. I picked flowers and searched for Indian arrowheads while he set up his tripod and surveyed the area .We discussed my findings as we sat on a rock and ate the sandwiches Mother packed in his black tin lunch box. We accumulated quite a collection of Yuchi, Wes toe, Saluda and Congaree tribe arrowheads, enhancing the books we read about South Carolina Indian tribes, their myths and legends. Those days included stopping at country stores for RC colas, peanut butter crackers, boiled peanuts, and Moon Pies.

Even after I was reading on my own, *Honey Bunch* and *The Bobbsey Twins,* my father continued to read to me when he returned home on weekends. We reviewed each adventure and the details in order for him to "catch up" with me. Then in my pre-teen years he seemed just as interested as I in Trixie Beldon and then in the Nancy Drew mysteries.

As a teenager, I resented his weekly absences and then his stern discipline on weekends, but we remained connected because of his persistent enthusiasm over whatever novel I was reading for pleasure or required reading for English classes. We shared a love for mysteries: Perry Mason and Agatha Christie.

Though I complained about Daddy's absence, I now realize that he appeared for every single special event without exception. On stage during a school play, band concert, piano recital, church program, or a choir performance, I saw him sitting in the audience front and center. I hated performing, but his quirky little smile kept me focused on him. I pretended that he and Mother were the only ones in the room.

My school projects were magic scenes: miniature rivers winding around trees and rocks, highlighting whatever my assignment was. I'm sure my teachers knew Daddy helped because I had no artistic ability whatsoever.

My master's thesis on the novels of James Gould Cozzens and my advisor, the novelist Madison Jones, whet his interest; we conversed through letters about the subject matter. He preferred English literature to American, stirring up frequent debates.

My father was there to guide me in every important life decision. I still have a stern letter from him when I wanted to resign in the middle of my first year of teaching. The letter was a loving one but also a lecture on responsibility. He reminded me of my student loan, apartment expenses, blah, blah, blah. He gave me no option, just as his father before him. I also have that letter Daddy wrote my grandfather from Clemson, then a military school, begging to come home. After all, he was only sixteen, having skipped two grades - as was common back on the 1920's. My grandfather's stern reply left no option either.

I often wonder if Daddy wished for another profession. His math strengths and his artistic hand at drawing made him a successful and well-respected engineer. However, his writing skills and his love for literature spoke volumes.

I don't know whether my love of reading came from the natural habit my father created or from the desire to be near and to connect with him. Nevertheless, he formed a lasting bond between us. Like a yo-yo our love of books pulled us back together even in times when we were at odds. He opened up the whole wide world to me. *"Richer than I you can never be/ I had a father and mother who read to me."* Strickland Gillard

A letter from Daddy

~ A SPECIAL LETTER ~

1. Notice the Post Date during World War 2

2. NO POSTAGE NEEDED ~ FREE

3. For those old enough to remember,
   we did not need a street address

Sunday Morning.

My dearest little Daughter,

I have been intending to write you but never seem to have time to do anything much except work. I have received your letters and you'll never understand just how much they mean to me. Mama wrote and told me that you had been writing with my fountain pen. You must be getting to be a big girl to be able to do that. I can hardly wait to see you. I have so many things to tell you. You must save up all the things you want me to do when I come home, and we'll start right in as soon as I get there. I was helping in the kitchen yesterday and they have a big machine that washes dishes. You just push a button, put the dishes in by the thousand and they come out all clean. Simple, isn't it? I guess I'll have to get Mama one after the war. When we can eat. Put the dishes in it, and Mama and I both can play with you. Would you

50

like that? Friday, all of the men here went for a walk. Walked down along the Potomac river. Had our guns with us, steel helmets on, leggings (on and eye) and packs on our backs. Someone told me the view was beautiful. I couldn't see it 'cause perspiration kept running in my eyes. It was only about six miles so ~~when I come home we'll really take~~ some walks. (Around the back yard). — I am sending you some chewing gum now and when I come home, I'll bring you some more — also a doll baby or something. Be sweet for Moma and Grand mama and tell them that anything of mine you want to play with or tear up, to let you do just as you please. I'll have to close now, but will write you again soon. ~~Kiss Moma and Grand mama for me and remember that~~ I love you so very, very much.

Your
Daddy.

THOSE EYES

I GLIMPSED HER FROM A DISTANCE as we walked down the cobbled, walled street. She peered out at us from the edge of a crumbling stone building. As we drew closer to the narrow alley, she stood motionless, a tiny, dirty little figure with dark eyes staring. Those eyes were not the eyes of a child.

She stood braced against the corner of the building as if prepared to run but curious enough to remain, stork-like. I guessed that she was about four years old, petite and thin. Her tangled hair was brown, her skin olive, though the dirt that smeared her arms, bare legs and feet made her appear yet darker.

We drew even with her, slowing our steps, hesitant to speak for fear of frightening her. Her eyes followed us, more serious than her facial expression which was solemn indeed. Her little dress, torn in several places, might have been pink in some distant past. Now it was a dingy gray with just a hint of blush clinging in memory. Her thin little hands gripped the edge of the wall, perhaps to brace herself before bolting.

These observations were a flash, insignificant at the time, because all I saw were those huge brown eyes in that dirty little face. They were not the eyes of a child at all. They shone no light, those gorgeous, chocolate saucers. They were full of pain and fear and hopelessness. Wise old eyes with knowledge of things we would probably never know stared at us.

As we passed by the child and her alleyway, I smiled but did not attempt to speak. She did not run. She clung to the wall as only her head turned to follow us moving down the street. Some distance away, I looked back and saw the little waif, unmoving, still watching us. Those eyes—I see them still.

Andy Oldham

Born and raised in the Louisiana, Andy Oldham has been privileged to experience a rich Southern heritage. He has collected stories and colloquial sayings his entire life enabling him to write his first novel, *Everlasting Cronies.* He writes inspirational articles for the Northside Sun newspaper and enjoys writing personal life stories.

<u>Favorite Quote</u>

Memoir isn't the summary of a life; it's a window into a life, very much like a photograph in its selective composition. It may look like a casual and even random calling up of bygone events. It's not; it's a deliberate construction.

~William Zinsser

ONE DELICIOUS MEMORY

THER WAS A TIME where I hated girls, especially the one next door; and when I looked forward to going hunting with Dad. The time I remember best was when I made myself sick on chocolate pie. The place was Simpson. Located in Vernon Parish, Louisiana, the population remains around five hundred. Dad was called there to pastor Simpson Church of God.

"Back-in-the-day," as we say in 2016, pastors invited other pastors, evangelists, or guest preachers to come to their church for week-long revivals. I enjoyed them for one particular reason: Food! Yup, that's right. The county folk loved to shower the guest minister with food, especially sweets. Now I was blessed to carry extra weight as a child—I still am. I guess it was occasions like this that added a few more pounds.

I was nine years old in the summer of 1959. The evangelist was Bill Livingston. He was a tall, slender man with a perfect head of white hair. Unlike my Dad who had little hair, his was combed to perfection with Brylcream ("a little dab'l do ya"). He had been a missionary somewhere, I don't know where, and was now speaking for a week in our church. Best of all, he was going to stay at our house—in my room.

I sat on the front porch patiently waiting. For what you asked? Food, of course! The townspeople would plates and bowls of butter beans, cornbread, and sweet potatoes. Fresh beef one day, pork chops the next. Sometimes a little venison would come as a welcome surprise. Oh my, I could not begin to describe the amount of food coming in. My job was to be the scout. Of course, I created the position; it was all mine. Being the scout meant I got to greet our neighbors and receive bowls and platters of food.

While they stood and talked to Dad and Reverend Livingston, I continued to the kitchen with the vittles. Though not a written job description, secret agent was part of the task. We had a guest and it was my job to protect him from harm and see just what everyone brought. We sure didn't want Reverend Livingston to get sick, now did we? I was really looking for one singular dish among one particular category of food.

Sweets galore! Yum! Lemon pie (yuck). Coconut pie, well, okay. Chocolate pie, where was it? There was never a chocolate pie. I was hurt. I was devastated that someone, anyone, would not bring this guest speaker a chocolate pie. Day after day I grew weary. Scouting was no longer any fun. No chocolate pie...no chocolate p...no choc....six days and the only thing that arrived was frustration. I had given up hope until the last day of the revival. I just knew the neighbors were saving the best for last. Before church, during church and after church, the plates arrived covered and ready for my inspection. Still, no chocolate pie. Disillusionment accompanied by dejection and annoyance set in.

That last Sunday evening I sat in church listening to the last sermon. I could only think of one thing and I knew it was not going to happen, until...well...the sermon was over. Bill Livingston began to thank everyone for such loving hospitality. The welcome was great; the responses to his messages each evening were amazing.

His last words were, "I cannot begin to tell you how incredible the food was each night." He went on and on about it. He made the congregation chuckle when he said he had gained ten pounds. The real laughter came with his last statement. "I need you to do me a favor, please. Andy has looked at the delicious food you brought each night. He was also disappointed every single day that there was never a chocolate pie. Will someone please bake Andy a chocolate pie this week?"

The entire church broke into laughter. I was on the floor and under the pew. His words showered me more attention than I have ever had and it was no drizzle either. I was drenched in torment and pesterin' for weeks. Oh, you ask, did anyone bring a chocolate pie? Well, of course, five of them—that week! Yes indeedy, I made myself sick on chocolate pie and I didn't mind one little bit. Praise God from whom all blessings flow!

HUNTING FIASCO

THE ADVENT OF FALL HUNTING had arrived. A light snow had fallen and melted the week before. My brother and I went hunting around Salamonie Reservoir in northern Indiana with my best friend Mo. We took Mo's new but used 4-wheel drive Chevy Blazer with gigantic mud tires, knowing that we could go anywhere we wanted. Driving down a gravel road we noticed a peaceful grouping of deep woods across an open field.

Mo decided with his *go-anywhere* vehicle to take a short cut across this pasture. No sooner had we started when our nostrils filled with that favorite country aroma that makes so many ask, "What is that smell?" Whoever farmed this land had just finished spreading the field with fertilizer. Now, not that kind you pick up at the farm co-op, mind you, rather that kind that comes out of the south end of a north-bound cow. Some folks call it the *Essence of Manure.*

We were about halfway across when Mo started to fight with the rear end of the Blazer. For some reason the *Essence* combined with the mud from the melted snow was exceptionally slick. The steering wheel moved quickly from left to right and back as he fought to keep all 400 horses on a straight path. The struggle was short lived and we found ourselves stuck. We looked at each other in confounded trepidation—the four-wheel drive was not turned on. This may date me, but at that time turning on the four-wheel drive was accomplished from the outside by turning the hub on each wheel. While stopped we found the small amount of wind given by driving with the windows down had blocked most of the nosegay of bitter pungencies. Because we were so dumb as to not lock the hubs, we received the blessings of unsavory suffocation.

Climbing out of the Blazer, we noticed an old beat-up farm truck swerving in the mud and up the hill toward us. The farmer was waving and shouting some unintelligible words, so we waved back. He stopped, pulled a rifle from the back window rack and cocked the chamber. He stomped in front of the vehicle and said, "You're trespassing on my land and I am gonna put a bullet right through your motor." All three of us assured him that we thought we were on public land and apologized for being there.

He continued to shout and blame when Mo interrupted, "Uh, sir, your truck is rolling backwards down the hill." The farmer ran waving the gun shouting, "I'll be right back!"

The thought to take advantage of the moment was inspired in each of us as we climbed in the now set 4-wheel drive Blazer and skedaddled across the pasture swerving toward the paved road. Each of us agreed that the sight of that shotgun in our face terrified us and we sped the sixty miles home to Anderson.

LABOR DAY

I SIT AND REMINISCE, trying to remember a time that made this day significant. There were so many holidays we celebrated mostly the same with bar-b-que chicken on the brick grill Papaw had built in his back yard in Baton Rouge. The adults prepared the meal while my brothers and cousins and I took turns cranking the homemade custard ice cream. I loved sucking a piece of salt ice, but only for a second or two.

No one else in the family remembers what happened Labor Day at the Louisiana Governor's Mansion in the late 1950's. I know it's not something I just conjured up. I know it happened; I was there. So I try with diligence to summon up these recollections so that I can convey them to you as unforgettable...for me anyway.

My family was one of musical inclinations. Somewhere along the line I got left out except for thoroughly enjoying the melodious sounds made by others. I guess that is why this memory is so important to me. Here I am summoning this tale, not a big tale now, mind you, but since I cannot remember all of the details, I reckon it does account for what I do remember.

Overlooking a small lake and surrounded by majestic live oaks stands one of Baton Rouge's most prized possessions. The stately mansion proves the glory of the great state of Louisiana. She is a beaut, for sure. She struts her Doric white columns with a great southern pride, and, like many of the plantations of the South, she is built with magnificence and attitude. It is from here I petition this one recollection of the past to come forward.

"A standing joke in many of Louisiana's small, country churches goes, "Well, there are two things we know how to do around here,

worship and eat!" Put the two together and you've got the country church tradition of all-day singing and dinner on the ground." (*louisianafolklife.org*)

Dinner on the grounds is a long-standing tradition in the South and is usually done after church on Sundays. This was a special occasion for a special holiday. Our arrival at the governor's mansion was early. We knew it was going to be a long day. The heat was relentless, but we knew it would be worth all the sweat, the bees and the flies to get one little morsel of that delicious southern cooking. There were people from all over the state and I think a few strangers from the North. But that's ok, it was time for them to discover they have never really eaten right anyway.

Every family brought a dish of some kind. Tables were set with various meats including wild game and fried chicken just bustin' with goodness. A variety of vegetables grown in large and small family gardens soaking in potluck were laid out end to end. Another table served up corn bread butter-shined so bright you could almost see yourself smile when you bent over to take a long whiff. My favorite was, of course, the dessert table. Cakes were okay but pie, now that was a boy's aspiration, especially when it came to the chocolate one. Oh, and there was always more than one. Yes, indeedy.

One of the things about a gathering of this sort was that it was not just the food. No sir. It was about so much more. Boys and girls spent the day playing games on the six-acre mansion's land. Some went fishin' in the lake. Most folks enjoyed the fellowship of friends and family and even new acquaintances. Recipes were swapped; singing practice took place wherever there was a guitar in the crowd. Some folk could be seen layin' on hands in prayer.

However, second only to the food was something really special. Groups from all over Louisiana came to sing. There were even some from other states who joined in this special day. I loved to watch my family most of all. You know, the ones, unlike me, that could actually sing and play instruments. My Uncle Edgar was always one to watch. His baldheaded little self was quite the show. He played his box guitar and sang with his brothers and sisters, one of whom was Uncle Dave Pearce,the state's Commissioner of Agriculture. He wore a harmonica holder around his neck and played that along with his guitar on some songs. He could surely lay out a whine that folks just loved to hear.

Other groups displayed fancy guitars, mandolins and fiddles. There were so many different instruments I was mesmerized. I especially loved the banjo pickin'; I promised myself I would learn to play that someday (Well, *someday* never has shown up). Combined with great piano playing, accordions and even a diddly-bow, there was music so wonderful I believe old Gabriel was blowing his horn along side the Father and the Son while they were dancin' with the saints. Now, put all of these instruments together with some great country gospel nasal, some good food and fellowship and all I can say is good gracious alive, heaven was on the grounds.

Like all memorable days this one had to come to an end. I have to admit it was an enjoyable day. I lay in the back window of the old Chevy, allowing the cool evening wind to blow through open windows, staring toward the mansion. When I enjoyed something I would watch it until it was out of sight. I wish I could remember more about this day, but this will have to do.

Singing in those days was more like what God put in His Word ~ *Make a joyful noise unto the Lord.* I guess I was the only one struck by the profound significance this day would have on my life. I am thankful for this memory, however, and will pass it on to those who follow.

THE NIGHT BESSIE BUMPED HER HEAD

HER DADDY WANTED A BOY so much. He announced that, irrespective of the gender, he was naming her John Neil. Her mom proclaimed that her name was going to be Ider regardless of what he named her. To settle the dispute they named her John Neil Ider Oldham. Everyone who knew her called her Ida. I called her Grannie.

One of the things I enjoyed most, in growing up in Louisiana, was going to her house in Pioneer during the summer time to spend a week, just the two of us. The summer of 1959, at nine years old, is one I have never forgotten. Pioneer, Louisiana, was a small town with two wood frame country stores. Only one had a gas pump. Because it was a farming community, there was always danger on every corner if you did not stay fully aware of your surroundings.

I was only four when Papa died in 1954. Grannie was left to tend the forty-acre farm alone. Once I reached the age of nine I began, as my older brother Bill had done years before, to visit her on the farm for a week each summer. I generally played outside during the day, exploring the woods and shooting my BB gun. Once in a while, when she had time to watch, Grannie would allow me to shoot the .22 rifle she kept by her bed. When the nights rolled around, the farmlands were dark and spooky.

A distressed fear arrived at nighttime. I knew I would be going to bed alone. I was terrified of the dark as a child. The country was no place for a boy afraid of black uncertainty. When a storm brewed, the air was ever changing, revealing an eerie and deficient comfort. Like a demon of obscurity ever watching for some little boy to step outside, I was vigilant to stay close to

Grannie. When she left the room so did I. Then there were those nights with no moon and a pure piece of black velvet stretched across the sky. Painted to the canopy were sprinkled millions of shiny diamonds and twinkling winks of colorful royalty. The nights I enjoyed the most were those when the moon was full. These nights brought a serene and placid tranquility to an otherwise somber outdoor uncertainty. Even though a peaceful evening, I was still afraid to go to bed alone.

One night I found myself reluctant to go to bed. I was thankful for the full moon that night. I climbed into Grannie's big feather bed. I was never sure if I really slept with her because I fell asleep while she watched the news—and found her making cathead biscuits and scrambled eggs when I woke each morning. Still, the thought that she really did sleep with me gave me some facsimile of security before succumbing to the back roads of a country night.

The moon was full. The sky revealed its brightness one minute and darkness the next as clouds were shoved around by a strong wind. I was in a peaceful sleep when awakened by a loud snort— I could hear it but I could not see it. The sound of heavy breathing conquered my soul and calm retreated. The moon suddenly brightened the room illuminating two large eyes. I sat straight up, gripped the covers to my nose—too scared to move. My heartbeat increased and tears began to flow as the muscles in my body stood at attention.

I could hear Grannie running down the hallway when all the anxiety a little boy could hold in released itself toward the window. The cry of bloody murder flew through the house and Bessie pulled her head up and bellowed like *I'm the one who scared her.* That old milk cow jerked her head back out of that window as fast as she could, tearing out the glass and the wood frame that held it in.

Grannie entered the room, ran to the window and stuck her head out shouting words that I did not hear. Bessie skedaddled back toward the barn where she belonged. Grannie turned to calm me down and found me aiming the .22 at the window. Another frightful sight was Grannie with no teeth, but I was relieved by her recognizable voice. I dropped the gun and climbed under the covers where I burst into tears. Grannie climbed in beside me, wrapped her arms around me and slept the rest the night, or least until I woke up to find her cooking cathead biscuits, scrambled eggs and grits.

THE DUMBEST THING I HAVE EVER DONE

THERE WERE TWO THINGS little boy's wanted in the 1950's. One was a pocketknife. He didn't feel like a man until he had a pocketknife just like his father and grandfather. The other was a BB gun. One summer my younger brother saved his money and purchased a Daisy Model 111-40 Red Ryder.

He was excited and ready to shoot just about anything. Taking his invitation to place cans on the fence in exchange for a turn to shoot, I joined in his excitement. Dad gave us strict instructions not to shoot until he returned from the store. My brother poured little gold BB's in the ammo hole. He scoped down the barrel and made peow, peow sounds.

I asked if I could try. I set the stock against my cheek and my eyes slid down the barrel to the tin can focused in the v-shaped site. It was like someone erased the blackboard of sensibility and the urge to pull the trigger possessed my very being. I wanted to be first to hear the ping of cans flying off the post.

I don't know what came over me when I pointed and yelled, "Look!" My little brother's eyes moved away and deceit placed the barrel on top of his barefoot big toe. Then I pulled the trigger.

Now, you may think that that was the dumbest, most hurtful thing, I could have done, and I agree, it was pretty bad, but let me continue. He screamed and he hollered and he cried and hopped around on one foot for I don't know how long.

"It couldn't have hurt that bad," I said.

The same courageous boldness that possessed Moses to get angry enough to kill that Egyptian soldier consumed my brother that morning. He stopped hopping around, and his tear-filled spirit looked me square in the eyes and said something that placed the fear of God, and of the devil all into one phrase.

"I'm gonna tell Dad."

I don't know about you, but with me, those words cut clear to the bone. Dad may have been a preacher, but the forty-four inch belt, called "Old Joe," around his waist was more powerful than dynamite. When Old Joe hit my backside it moved me so much that, if the skin hadn't held in the flesh it would splatter like a million stones off the side of a mountain.

Shooting his big toe was pretty dumb, huh? Conversely, it was not the dumbest thing I ever did. My next few words filled that hallmark. "If you won't tell Dad, I'll let you shoot *my* toe."

I screamed, and hollered, and cried and hopped around on one foot. I felt like what he called me, the biggest imbecile in the world.

We didn't hear Dad's arrival. When he heard our story he was shocked, but not surprised. Dad agreed my stupidity and pain was enough punishment and Old Joe stayed on his waist. I did have that to be thankful for anyway.

WOOOPS!

MY SON GOT UP EARLY and joined me this morning. We chatted about Saturday's game at Southern Miss. We sipped a little coffee and laughed together about the game. I was reminded of when I played football. At sixty-four, that seems so long ago.

I attended Stephen F. Austin High School in Houston, TX. I played defensive nose guard and was also the long punt center. As a nose guard I was the antagonist. My job was to harass, intimidate and literally destroy the opposing center's confidence while he was hiking the ball. I told him there was nothing he could do to keep me from charging right through him to take out the quarterback. I would knock him on his butt and it would be his fault they lost yardage. I swung my forearm in his face to terrorize and convince him that he was a failure.

Then I laughed when I remembered the first time I hiked that long ball for a punt. In my face was the biggest, ugliest, defensive nose guard I'd ever seen. He was force-feeding me a bucket of fear and discouragement. His battle-worn arm displayed scrapes and bruises proving his proficiency. I was now the recipient of the same fear tactics I had used on others.

I told him he wasn't getting through me. My heart was determined on taking care of this ape. I took that nose guard straight to the ground. *There*, I thought, *he won't try that again*. When he jumped up laughing and pointing behind me I turned around to see a pile of players covering the ball. Because I was fixated on my opponent instead of my job, I had created a hole in the line for others to run through, and the ball had only gone about four yards.

I had lost focus and taken my eyes off of what was important. I realized then that it was not about my fear, but about the team. I had let the team down because I was afraid of my opponent. Oh yes, I had proved I could take him to the ground but I really hadn't beaten him. The opposing team was in possession of the ball on the twelve-yard line. Do you know how I felt? It was *my* fault.

I dragged my tail to the sidelines. No one said a word, but I could feel the terror of the let down. Two plays later our opponents put seven points on the scoreboard. Coach Russo came over and stood by me without saying a word. Another punt situation had arrived. Without looking at me, he asked two simple questions.

"Do you have that out of your system now?

"Yesser,"

"Do you know what to do next?"

"Yes Sir!"

"Then go out there and prove yourself."

I knew he believed in me and that if we were to win I must give my best. Not doing so would put a heavier load on my team members. I hiked the ball, the punter kicked it and I had done my job.

Football is only a memory now. Even though it was my first time to hike the ball, I failed. I was happy Coach had not given me a chewing I deserved. We played hard throughout the game. At the end of that game we left the field with a loss. The only defeat of the year. I look back now and realize we would have had a perfect season if not for my blunder.

This packrat has learned that what the next generation will value most is not what we owned, but the evidence of who we were and the tales of how we loved. In the end, it's the family stories that are worth the storage.
-Ellen Goodman,
The Boston Globe

Vivian Newkirk

Vivian retired from high school teaching in 1995. She enrolled in a night course in writing and has continued to specialize in family stories. She also enjoys genealogy, movies, and reading thrillers. She is a member of the Gulf Coast Writers Association where her work has appeared in its quarterly magazine. She won first place in an Alabama Conclave contest in 2014 for her submission of a creative nonfiction story.

<u>Favorite Quote</u>

We are all in a craft in which no one is a master.
~ Ernest Hemingway

TUBERCULOSIS SCARE

I WAS SIX YEARS OLD in 1940 when my mother withdrew me from first grade one April morning at the local Catholic school. I didn't question her motives; I was an obedient child. I'm not sure she told me why. I often left school for the day to visit this doctor or that one to find the root of my illnesses. I was unaware this latest trip would take me away for months.

I recall a long drive past fields and thick woods from Jackson some forty miles south on Highway 49. We crossed a railroad track west of the highway and entered a beautiful area with buildings sitting along a winding road. A kind lady met us in front of a brick building and said her name was Miss Effie. She took me in hand and led me to a large room filled with beds. Frightened, I wondered why Mother had brought me to a hospital. She pointed to a tall bed, "That's yours, Dear." she said. Miss Effie handed me a pair of white panties and instructed me to remove my flowered dress and white shoes. I obeyed and put my clothes in a nearby cabinet Miss Effie called a locker. Mother had left two pairs of pajamas, bedroom slippers, and a robe to add to the interior. Six months later I redressed in my pretty outfit when I left this place called the Preventorium. It adjoined the Sanatorium, where tuberculosis patients received treatment.

The women on duty had us moving on a schedule of napping, playing, eating, and studying. Discipline was strict with fifty little kids ages four to twelve in one confined area. The outdoors was our playground, as fresh air and sunshine were important. Every week nurses took our temperature, weighed us and often gave us an X-ray, the only way to detect TB. When I arrived I weighed twenty-five pounds. A visiting medical team checked

72

our progress each month. Health officials believed sickly, undernourished children were targets for tuberculosis. The solution was special care and isolation from daily public life for a period of time.

Our playground had a swimming pool, a play village, a duck pond, and outdoor gym sets. We thought only rich kids were this lucky. We played happily, only wishing to see our family more often. Visitors Day was twice monthly.

Our daily schedule allowed for school studies in the mornings, outside play, then a fat-rich meal followed by an hour's rest. We drank fresh milk at our meals and between play times.

The radio was our connection to the outside world. I recall hearing Kate Smith sing "God Bless America" one rainy day when we played indoors in the "round room." Indoor time gave us plentiful toys and books to enjoy quietly. During nap time or sleep for the night, we had to lie on our backs with our eyes closed. This didn't make us fall asleep any quicker, as the large windows behind our beds provided brilliant light from the afternoon sun and summer evening light until late. A lot of peeping and snickering went on, I remember.

In mid-August Mother received the message of my release. She came that afternoon. My clothing was a bit tight from having gained twenty-five pounds. I was TB free. When I returned home and entered school again, I kept my time away a secret. I was afraid the kids might not be my friends if I told them where I had lived for six months. As I grew to adulthood I was unaware of hundreds of other previous patients holding onto their own secrets. When my children were old enough to understand, I told them about living away from home. After that, I found it easier to share my story.

A few years ago one former patient began a FaceBook page searching for information for a book. Soon many "friends" joined, former patients on the Magee campus. The stigma of their past no longer haunted them. They became eager to add their memories and snapshots and reconnect with friends. Occasional reunions on the campus renew memories now shared with spouses and adult offspring.

The Mississippi Preventorium continued accepting patients until the mid-1960s. The campus is now the Boswell Regional Center, aiding people with developmental issues.

THE ARGUMENT

"I WILL NOT SIT ON A PAINT BUCKET, PERIOD."

"It's only for the summers, Hon," I pleaded.

"You heard me, no paint bucket." Dick folded his arms and thrust his chin defiantly. This was our first retirement argument.

 We had a newly-built cabin in the lower Catskills with a separate bath house containing an old tub large enough for a midget. Missing was a toilet. Living off the grid meant no electricity or running water. After checking the Internet, the five-gallon plastic paint bucket was our only choice, unless Dick forked out big bucks for a commercial compost toilet.

"The bucket is a home-made compost toilet. With a toilet seat to replace the top, we layer the bucket with scraps: torn newspapers, crumbled leaves, sawdust, kitchen scraps. Each time we use the bucket, we layer. Never an odor. When full, we top it and place in the sun in the side yard and start with a fresh bucket." I sounded like an advertisement

"So, what happens when we leave in the fall? Will we have forty buckets lining the property?" I knew Dick was pushing the subject.

"Maybe, but look at the compost you'll have for the garden next summer."

"How will our friends react when they enter the bath house and confront this bucket?"

"Now what friends of ours will make the trip from their amenities in Mississippi to stay in the deep woods with no television?"

Our Toilet

I'd made the suggestion to build the cabin. Dick felt he'd camped enough as a kid, but in time he consented to let me have my way.

I quit arguing and said nothing when he ordered a medium-sized compost toilet. The following summer he installed it *with help of a plumber* near the door of the bathhouse. Its plastic -molded form looked out of place in the woods. With the seating area four and a half feet high, we had to climb a step stool to sit. As the summer wound down, Dick discovered the non-electric wonder worked exactly like the five gallon paint bucket.

I smiled all summer. His decision cost time, money, and energy. The New York summers failed to produce enough heat to compost the large refuse basin. Cleaning was more complicated. What a grumbling summer that was!

MISS VELSOR, PEGGY AND ME

Miss VELSOR'S DANCE STUDIO sat on the second floor of a commercial building on South Lamar Street in Jackson, Mississippi. Mother and I trudged up the narrow stairway squeezed between a restaurant and a plumbing supply business. While she enrolled me for ballet and tap lessons, I looked around the vast room. A mirror the size of our school auditorium faced the entrance. Bars ran the length of the two walls. A flutter played an imaginary piano inside my stomach. I was about to begin dance lessons in this very room.

Miss Gladys Velsor danced as she walked. She twirled and posed to show us how a dancer used her body. She exuded mystery dressed gypsy style in long, colorful skirts and full-sleeved blouses. When she waved her arms, the sleeves widened like petals of a sunflower. She pinned her dark hair off her face. She smiled, only appearing serious when she wielded her companion, a long pointer, at a leg or foot out of place. We fifth grade girls listened to her every word.

One afternoon during ballet class she read a letter sent by a Hollywood movie company to dancing teachers everywhere. A search was on for an experienced dancer at least eighteen years old. "Now, students, this shows you how persistence and hard work may one day give you the chance to enter a contest like this." I rode the bus home imagining my winning such a prize.

Near the end of the year Miss Velsor announced the contest winner as Peggy Middleton of Canada. At that time we had no idea how she would enter our adult lives.

My dream of a dancing career faded as I entered ninth grade. Like girls of the mid 1940s, I wrote fan letters and read magazines like *Movie Star* and *Photoplay.* In one issue I found an article on Peggy Middleton who by then had a "Hollywood name." I copied the movie company's address and wrote her a fan letter on my best notebook paper. Within a month she responded with five black and white glossies of her dressed in her costume for her first movie, "Scheherazade." She was beautiful with curly hair falling to her waist. On one photo she wrote," To Vivian" and signed her name. That cemented our connection. I was her fan forever.

Ten years later on the night before my wedding, I pulled out my collection of fan photos and tore them, saying goodbye to my youth, goodbye to Gene, Roy, Sons of the Pioneers, Bing Crosby, and others I've forgotten. I gazed a long time debating whether to keep or destroy those from Peggy.

One evening in 1965 as my children watched "The Addams Family," I interjected during the advertising. I thought it a good time to tell the story of the set of particular fan photos. They gushed, "Oh Mom, how could you?" when I told them five of the photos I destroyed were from the actress they were watching play the role of the popular Morticia: Yvonne de Carlo.

LESSONS IN ORGANIC GARDENING

NOWADAYS SHOPPERS PURCHASE ORGANIC FOOD. Outdoor markets abound in cities and small towns with fresh fruits and vegetables. However, as early as 2000 I'd never heard of fingerling potatoes, heirloom tomatoes, and hand-me-down seeds. In short, I was no cook.

I clerked several summers in upstate New York in my son's store KUDZU in a converted gas station. Inside lay a tempting variety of goods; outside where gas pumps once sat were trays of organic vegetables on ice.

One Saturday morning a new customer called me over and asked about the vegetables. "Where do you get these?" she held up a bunch of greens. "From Washington Square. My son buys every Saturday morning and brings them to the store." I replied, as though saying Washington Square was a magic location. Weekends it is the melting pot of farmers who travel hundreds of miles to display their wares.

I learned her name was Andrea and she was starting her own garden. "Perhaps you'll want to buy from me next summer." I promised I'd check on her then. I was used to Mississippi's long growing season. However, I learned this area of New York produced vegetables and fruit from early August into fall; a long wait for a tomato sandwich.

The following June I visited her new garden. She had a farmhouse surrounded by acres of fallow land. On the south side of the house she had tilled the soil into tiny humps, perfect to cuddle the seeds while they germinated. A chill permeated the air as I stood outside while Andrea described her planting map.

"Let me show you what I've already done. Here are the peas whose vines will have to be supported; over there against the fence will be the first arugula and spinach; at the opposite end will be patches of tomatoes." She visualized a full-grown garden; I saw rumpled dirt.

Every Tuesday I drove into her driveway in the early hours, long before the sun raised its head. Every visit was a lesson shared. I looked forward to learning what I'd never known: the distinct fragrance of arugula and why the fragrance disappeared after shipment; how to recognize varieties of lettuce; how sunflowers crossed-pollinated and the height they reach before cutting; how fingerling potatoes, resembling arthritic fingers, were roasted a century ago by the Lenape Indians of the Delaware region.

Andrea was a walking encyclopedia. One morning after a series of rains, we donned boots and stepped gently over rows to reach a budding plant. Andrea recited non-stop her favorite cooking techniques and shortcuts, her use of herbal seasonings. "You must try fava beans," she insisted and ran through the recipe as though my mind was a stenographer's machine. She emphasized planting heirloom seeds rather than those sold in packages.

Often we sat on a nearby bench in the garden as though expecting a bell to tinkle when a vegetable grew an inch. Sometimes we pulled weeds. One morning I confessed my inability to cook. "I'm excellent at opening cans and packages and warming their contents." She assured me cooking was enjoyable with a few ideas. She pointed to patches of vegetables that would cook well in the same pot and served as one dish.

One early July morning an overjoyed voice greeted me as I opened the car door. "The peas are up; oh Viv, come see the green tops on the carrots, and look, buds on the tomato plants." We heralded the sight of the green leaf buds pushing their way through the soil to bathe in the sunlight. Somewhat like cooing over our babies as they opened their eyes to see the world for the first time. On one occasion Andrea had me walk to an unknown patch in the side yard. "Run your hand into the dirt and wander until you touch something; tell me what you feel." As my fingers pawed through the dirt I hit some odd shapes. I shrieked, "I found something. I don't know what it is!"

"Potatoes. Can you find the different shapes under there?" We laughed as I touched this one and that one. "These potatoes have been handed down from one generation to another. The odder they are the more original." She had as much fun with my discoveries as I did.

By August the weather had warmed. Salad greens, onions, carrots and tomatoes were ready for picking. After Andrea showed me how to properly pick the produce and cut the sunflower stems, I was on my own. I began as early as six o'clock on Friday mornings. A basket lay at the gate. I hooked it onto my arm and walked up and down the rows gathering the vegetables needed for the store at nine o'clock. Those mornings I reveled in the silence: no blaring televisions, no busy traffic on the road nearby, no children playing. All I heard were chirping birds and cackling hens.

When I completed my rounds, I walked into her kitchen where she was finishing breakfast. This was weighing time. As she weighed each item she noted the pounds and ounces on a slip of paper. If there were extra eggs, I'd order six dozen. Nothing like a fresh egg direct from its source to perk up a meal.

I left for home in September when pumpkins crawled from under their leafy vines, a new crop of spinach reached for sunlight, and new potatoes stretched their bodies underground. I took with me a memory of moments when my senses awoke to the beauty and fragrance of an organic garden.

MY FIRST WATCH

I WAS FOUR YEARS OLD IN 1935 when Mother bought me a Mickey Mouse watch. She was a clerk at Woolworth's and bought the watch at a discount from its $3.25 marked price. The Ingerrsoll Company sold these wind-up watches as early as 1933.

On the face of the watch Mickey pointed out the hours and minutes with his yellow gloved hands as he stood on skinny legs in his oversize red shoes. I felt grown up when I learned to buckle the black band onto my arm. I knew no one else my age with a watch as fine as this. Like Mother's watch, Mickey had a real crystal cover protecting him. That crystal was my downfall.

On numerous occasions when we visited my grandparents' home in South Mississippi, I found an adventure I often repeated. Having no playmate in the large house, I played "pretend" under beds. I looked for lost treasure, hid from robbers, discovered how to escape from bad men while squiggling on my stomach in the low space. Mickey stayed close and helped me escape from danger. On one tense exploration I heard a Crack! Mick took a bullet. Even with the broken crystal he stayed with me. I crawled out from the depths of the cave to civilization with bits of glass clinging to my wrist.

In the kitchen Mother and her family talked softly. I walked past those uncles and aunts all the time worrying I'd never see Mick again. Mother examined the damage and calmly said, "Don't worry, we can get Mr. Bourgeois to put on a new crystal." Mick stayed in the "hospital" for nearly a week. My left arm felt as bare as my dad's bald head. Mother suggested I tighten the strap, thinking that was my problem. She didn't know how the crystal broke. Until I had Mick back with me, my adventures weren't as interesting. No one could read the map or open locks or use his big eyes to tell me where to go in the darkness.

When Mick returned, I took special care of him. I wiped his face and wound him every night before I went to bed. He slept in his box on the bedside table. I never failed to say "Goodnight, Mickey." I imagined he replied "G'night, Viv."

Did I learn my lesson after that first break? No. I broke the crystal three times more before Mother caught on to my underworld adventures. She put Mickey away in her secret place. I didn't see him again until I was six when I was too big to slip under beds.

Made in the USA
San Bernardino, CA
13 September 2016